Do I Bug You?

A "Who Am I?" Book

THE SAN FRANCISCO
SCHOOL COLLECTION

Products marked with The San Francisco School
seal are developed using the principle that children
learn through play. University Games and The San
Francisco School are working together to create
products that engage and teach children. We adopt
techniques that work in the classroom and modify
them so they can be enjoyed by families.

ACKNOWLEDGMENTS

Special thanks to Ruth Cardillo, Karen Goodkin and the children of the San Francisco School.

© 2006 University Games

First edition published in 2006

University Games Corporation
2030 Harrison Street San Francisco CA 94110

University Games Europe B.V.
Australielaan 52 6199AA Maastricht Airport Netherlands

University Games Australia
10 Apollo Street Warriewood 2102 Australia

Library of Congress Cataloging-in-Publication Data on file with the publisher

ISBN: 1-57528-898-2

Printed in China

1 2 3 4 5 6 7 8 9 10 - 09 08 07 06 05

I usually have two sets of wings and a hard shell covering.

Who am I?

I like to eat ant poop.

Ancient Egyptians worshiped me.

I am a
Beetle

I make the loudest sound of all insects.

Who am I?

I can lay between four to six hundred eggs.

I cool myself by sweating.

I am a
Cicada

I am the only insect that has
two wings.

I spit my food back up before
I swallow it.

I have 4000 lenses in each eye.

Who am I?

I am a

Fly

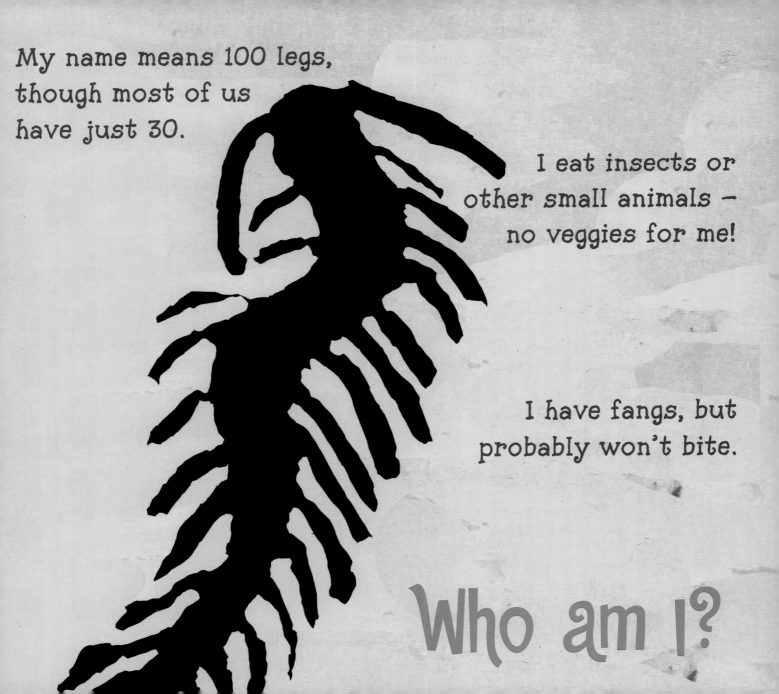

My name means 100 legs, though most of us have just 30.

I eat insects or other small animals — no veggies for me!

I have fangs, but probably won't bite.

Who am I?

I can hold my breath for up to 40 minutes.

I can live a long time without my head.

I am one of the oldest animals on Earth.

Who am I?

I am a
Cockroach

I can fly at speeds up to 30 miles per hour.

I catch flies with my
sharp jaws.

I can see behind me.

Who am I?

I am a
Dragonfly

I chew from side to side
rather than up and down.

My spots fade as
I get older.

My bright colors scare
off enemies.

Who am I?

I am a
Ladybug

I make honey inside my home, called a hive.

I never sleep—
not even at night.

Who am I?

Sometimes I have hair on my eyes.

I can jump several feet
in the air.

I have five eyes and
no ears.

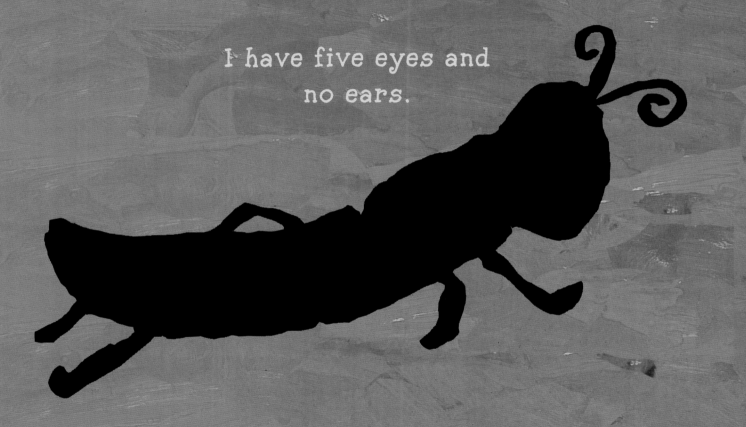

My blood is green.

Who am I?

I am a
Grasshopper

I can breathe underwater.

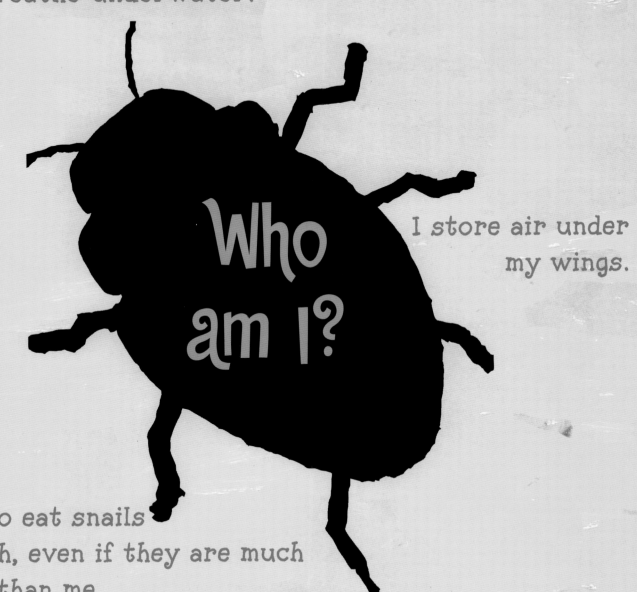

Who am I?

I store air under my wings.

I like to eat snails and fish, even if they are much bigger than me.

I am a
Diving Beetle

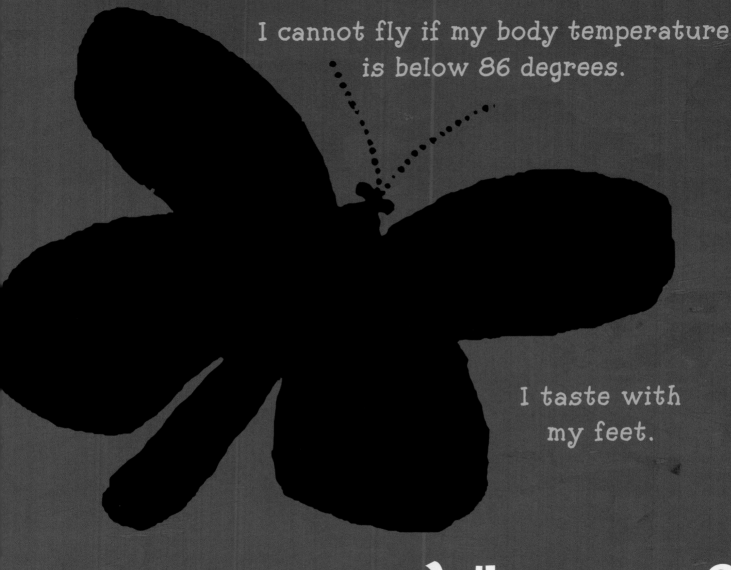

I cannot fly if my body temperature is below 86 degrees.

I taste with my feet.

Sometimes my tongue is as long as my body.

Who am I?

I am a
Butterfly

I can carry up to 20 times my own weight.

Each of my two eyes is made of many smaller eyes.

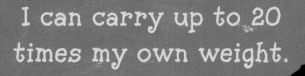

Who am I?

I have a very large brain for my size.